AMAZING MOMENTS IN

Tennis TITAN!

Serena Williams at Wimbledon in 2002

By James Buckley Jr.
Illustrated by Chris Fowler

BEARPORT
PUBLISHING

BEAR CLAW

Minneapolis, Minnesota

Credits

Cover art by Tom Rogers. Photos: 21 top © Luke Jevans/Dreamstime.com; 21 bottom © Zhukovsky/Dreamstime.com; 22 © Sven Simon/Picture Alliance/Newscom; 23 © Zhukovsky/Dreamstime.com.

Bearport Publishing Company Product Development Team
President: Jen Jenson; Director of Product Development: Spencer Brinker; Managing Editor: Allison Juda; Associate Editor: Naomi Reich; Senior Designer: Colin O'Dea; Associate Designer: Elena Klinkner; Associate Designer: Kayla Eggert; Product Development Specialist: Anita Stasson

Produced by Shoreline Publishing Group LLC
Santa Barbara, California
Designer: Patty Kelley
Editorial Director: James Buckley Jr.

DISCLAIMER: This graphic story is a dramatization based on true events. It is intended to give the reader a sense of the narrative rather than a presentation of actual details as they occurred.

Library of Congress Cataloging-in-Publication Data

Names: Buckley, James, Jr., 1963- author. | Fowler, Chris illustrator.
Title: Tennis titan! : Serena Williams at Wimbledon in 2002 / by James
   Buckley Jr. ; illustrated by Chris Fowler.
Description: Minneapolis, MN : Bearport Publishing Company, [2024] |
   Series: Amazing moments in sports | Includes bibliographical references
   and index.
Identifiers: LCCN 2023005616 (print) | LCCN 2023005617 (ebook) | ISBN
   9798885099912 (library binding) | ISBN 9798888221730 (paperback) | ISBN
   9798888223062 (ebook)
Subjects: LCSH: Williams, Serena--1981---Juvenile literature. | Wimbledon
   Championships (116th : 2002 : Wimbledon, London, England)--Juvenile
   literature. | Women tennis players--United States--Biography--Juvenile
   literature.
Classification: LCC GV994.W55 B83 2024 (print) | LCC GV994.W55 (ebook) |
   DDC 796.342092 [B]--dc23/eng/20230213
LC record available at https://lccn.loc.gov/2023005616
LC ebook record available at https://lccn.loc.gov/2023005617

For more information, write to Bearport Publishing, 5357 Penn Avenue South, Minneapolis, MN 55419.

CONTENTS

Chapter 1
THE ROAD TO WIMBLEDON

JULY 6, 2002
WIMBLEDON TENNIS CHAMPIONSHIP
LONDON, ENGLAND

Serena Williams walked onto Centre Court at the All England Club. She was about to play in the final at the most famous tennis tournament in the world. She was one match away from her first Wimbledon title.

Serena was one of the rising stars in women's tennis. She was also one of the few professional Black players in the sport. She knew that millions of little girls saw her as an inspiration.

Here are the finalists for the **Singles** Championship.

From the United States... Serena Williams.

I'VE MADE IT THIS FAR. NOW, ALL I HAVE TO DO IS BEAT MY SISTER.

Also from the United States... Venus Williams!

Serena and Venus had come a long way to reach this important tennis match. When they were growing up in Compton, California, their father taught them to play tennis.

OKAY, GIRLS, WE'RE ALMOST THERE. JUST WATCH OUT FOR THE BROKEN GLASS ON THE COURTS.

Despite some difficulties for the family, Richard Williams thought becoming tennis stars would be a way for his daughters to succeed.

He made the girls work hard.

GOOD WORK! THAT'S RIGHT— USE YOUR STRENGTH!

They soon got very good, and they loved playing together!

NICE GAME, VENUS!

YEAH, BUT I WAS BETTER, RIGHT?

Venus started playing tournaments first. She dominated, using a powerful **serve** to win game after game.

When she turned eight, Serena began playing in tournaments, too.

Like her sister, she won a lot!

Because Venus was older, the girls didn't play against each other... yet.

NICE TROPHY, SIS!

YOU, TOO! WAY TO WIN!

In 1991, the family moved to Florida, where the girls attended a tennis academy.

California

Florida

After several years at the academy, both girls turned pro. That meant that they would play against the best in the world, plus they could be paid for winning!

HERE WE GO!

But turning pro meant the sisters would sometimes have to play each other. At first, Venus won most of their matches.

But at the 1999 U.S. Open, Serena won the sisters' first **Grand Slam** singles title.

Then, Venus won the famous Wimbledon title in 2000. She became the first Black player to be ranked No. 1 in the world!

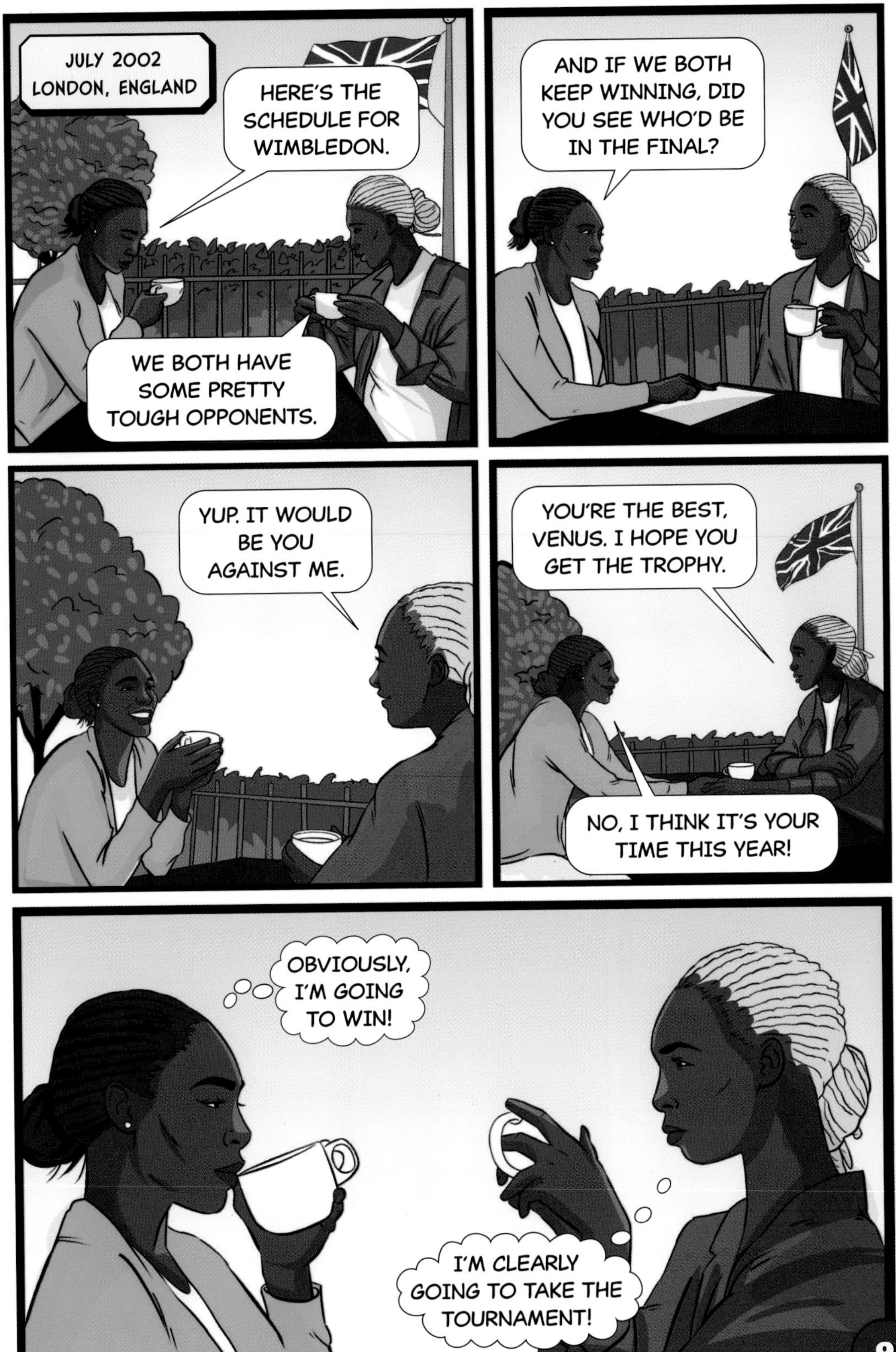
JULY 2002
LONDON, ENGLAND
HERE'S THE SCHEDULE FOR WIMBLEDON.
WE BOTH HAVE SOME PRETTY TOUGH OPPONENTS.
AND IF WE BOTH KEEP WINNING, DID YOU SEE WHO'D BE IN THE FINAL?
YUP. IT WOULD BE YOU AGAINST ME.
YOU'RE THE BEST, VENUS. I HOPE YOU GET THE TROPHY.
NO, I THINK IT'S YOUR TIME THIS YEAR!
OBVIOUSLY, I'M GOING TO WIN!
I'M CLEARLY GOING TO TAKE THE TOURNAMENT!

Chapter 2

SISTER VS. SISTER

Venus was given the No. 1 **seed** in the tournament. She would have to win six matches to reach the finals. In the first couple of rounds, she mowed down her opponents!

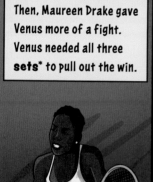

Then, Maureen Drake gave Venus more of a fight. Venus needed all three **sets*** to pull out the win.

Next, she lost only two games to Elena Likhovtseva on her way to victory!

A win over Justine Henin in the **semifinal** round sent Venus into the championship.

*In tennis, players need to win six games to win a set. At Wimbledon, women need two sets to win the match.

Serena was seeded No. 2. She made it to the finals without losing a single set!

In the third round, she battled to win two **tiebreakers** over Els Callens.

Serena defeated Chanda Rubin in the fourth round.

Then, Serena easily beat Amelie Mauresmo in her semifinal match.

That set up a sister vs. sister battle!

The 2002 match would be the first time since 1884 that sisters had met in a Grand Slam final.

LILIAN WATSON

MAUD WATSON

The sports world was excited about the big match. Everyone wanted to hear what the sisters thought would happen.

WHAT'S IT LIKE PLAYING YOUR SISTER?

WILL YOU COME OUT ON TOP, SERENA?

THE CHAMPIONSHIPS WIMBLEDON

NO MATTER WHAT HAPPENS, I LOVE MY SISTER! BUT I HOPE I WIN!

I LOVE MY SISTER, TOO! BUT THAT TROPHY WILL BE MINE!

From the start of the match, Serena made Venus chase shots from side to side.

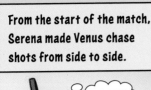

WOW...

SHE'S...

ON... FIRE!

But Venus hung in there. Serena made mistakes that let her sister win games.

Both sisters won six games in the first set. They took a rest before playing a dramatic tiebreaker!

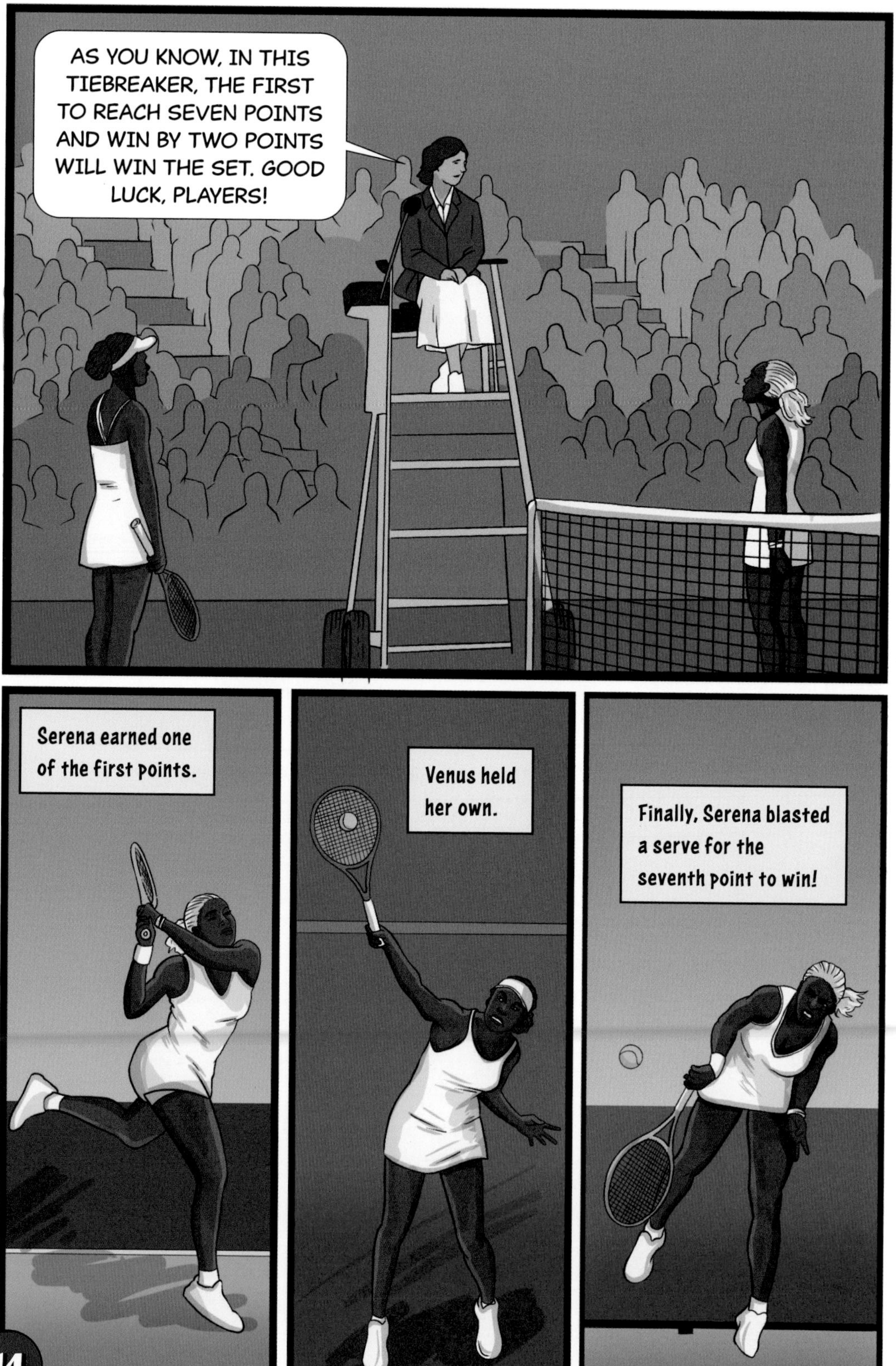
AS YOU KNOW, IN THIS TIEBREAKER, THE FIRST TO REACH SEVEN POINTS AND WIN BY TWO POINTS WILL WIN THE SET. GOOD LUCK, PLAYERS!
Serena earned one of the first points.
Venus held her own.
Finally, Serena blasted a serve for the seventh point to win!

As the second set began, Serena's serve—one of the fastest ever in women's tennis—was just too powerful for Venus.

Serena seemed to be getting stronger as the games went on.

YIKES!

Serena was determined to win. She didn't let playing her sister slow her down!

Finally, Serena had just one more game to win. And it was her turn to serve!

15

Chapter 3

SERENA THE CHAMPION

The Wimbledon fans let Serena know they loved her.

LET'S GO, SERENA!

YOU CAN DO IT!

JUST ONE MORE POINT!

MATCH POINT. QUIET, PLEASE.

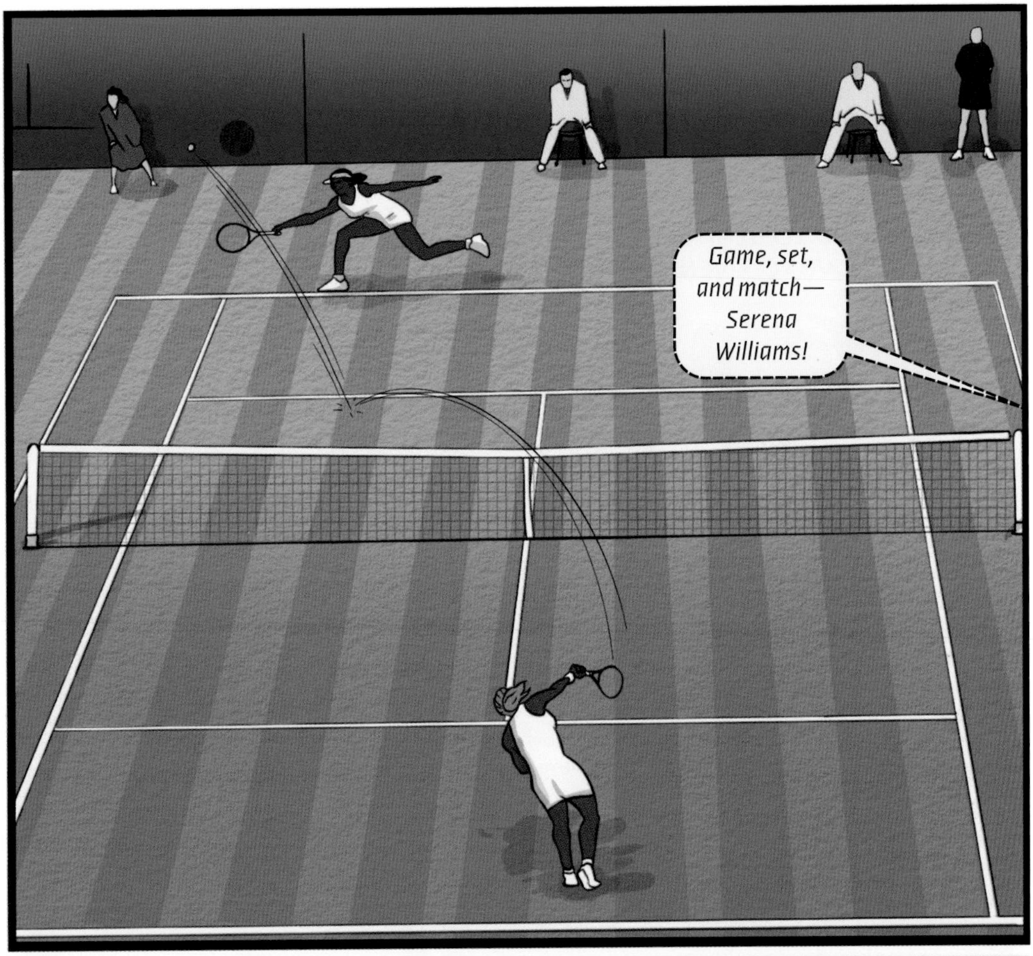
Game, set, and match— Serena Williams!

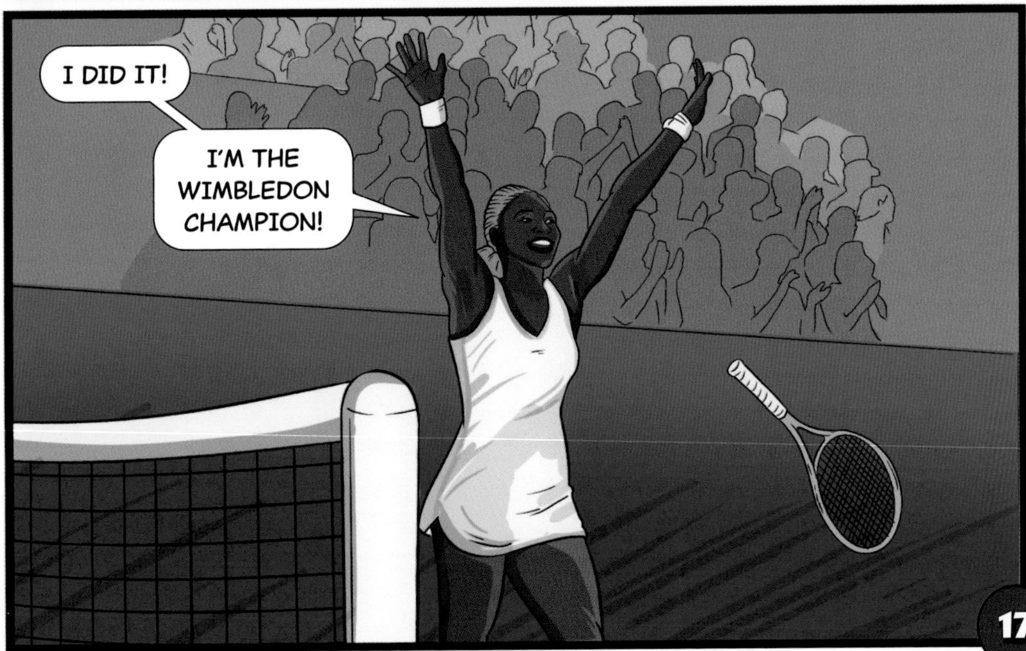
I DID IT!
I'M THE WIMBLEDON CHAMPION!

CONGRATULATIONS, SERENA! I'M PROUD OF YOU.

I'M JUST SORRY I HAD TO BEAT YOU! LOVE YOU, VENUS!

As the sisters made their way to the center of the court for the trophy ceremony, Venus shared a tip.

REMEMBER, YOU HAVE TO **CURTSY** TO THE ROYALTY!

GOT IT! THANKS, BIG SIS!

Serena accepted her Wimbledon trophy from England's Princess Anne.

After her big win at Wimbledon, Serena moved to No. 1 in the world rankings. It was the start of the greatest career in women's tennis history!

Venus went on to win seven Grand Slam singles. She also teamed with Serena to win four Olympic gold medals for **doubles**.

Serena kept piling up championship after championship. By the time she retired in 2022, she had won an incredible 23 Grand Slam singles titles. At one point, she was champion of all four Grand Slams at once.

The "little" Williams sister had become the Greatest of All Time!

GRAND SLAMS

Each year, the best women's tennis players in the world take part in the four Grand Slam events. They are considered the most important tournaments of the season. Players want to win them more than any others. The four Grand Slams are usually played in the same order every year.

Australian Open
Location: Melbourne Park, Melbourne, Australia
First Played: 1922
Most Women's Singles Titles: Margaret Court, 11

French Open
Location: Roland-Garros, Paris, France
First Played: 1897
Most Women's Singles Titles: Chris Evert, 7

Wimbledon
Location: All England Lawn Tennis and Croquet Club, London, England
First Played: 1884
Most Women's Singles Titles: Martina Navratilova, 9

U.S. Open
Location: Billie Jean King National Tennis Center, New York, New York
First Played: 1887
Most Women's Singles Titles: Molla Bjursedt Mallory, 8

The Wimbledon tournament is played on grass courts.

French Open events are held on courts made from clay.

OTHER SLAM STARS

Chris Evert

Evert was a tennis star from a young age. Over her career, she won 18 Grand Slam singles titles. From 1974 until 1986, she won at least one Grand Slam each year. Her best tournament was the French Open, where she won a record seven championships.

Martina Navratilova

This left-handed star was a top player for more than 30 years. Navratilova won 18 Grand Slam singles tournaments. She also held 31 doubles and 10 mixed doubles titles for a total of 59 Grand Slams. Her nine championships at Wimbledon are the most ever.

Steffi Graf

Graf was ranked No. 1 for a total of 377 weeks during her great career—the most ever. During that time, she won 22 Grand Slam singles titles. In 1988, she became the first woman to win all four Grand Slams in a single year.

Steffi Graf

GLOSSARY

curtsy to bend your knees in greeting to a royal person

doubles tennis played with two against two

Grand Slam one of the four major tennis tournaments held each year

match point the score that clinches a victory for a player in tennis

seed a ranking used in tennis tournaments with low numbers going to the best players

semifinal the match just before the last round of a tournament

serve the tennis stroke that begins each point

sets groups of games in tennis; winning six games wins a set

singles tennis played with one player against another

tiebreakers extra play to determine who will win a set when games are tied at six each

INDEX

READ MORE

Adamson, Thomas K. *Serena Williams (Torque: Sports Superstars).* Minneapolis: Bellwether Media, 2023.

Ahrens, Niki. *Serena Williams: Tennis Superstar (Boss Lady Bios).* Minneapolis: Lerner Publications, 2022.

Leslie, Jay. *Game, Set, Sisters! The Story of Venus and Serena Williams (Who Did It First?).* New York: Henry Holt and Company, 2021.

LEARN MORE ONLINE

1. Go to **www.factsurfer.com** or scan the QR code below.
2. Enter **"Tennis Titan"** into the search box.
3. Click on the cover of this book to see a list of websites.